Norbert Braun

DAWNING

OF A NEW ERA

**An Attempt to Escape
the Strangling Grip
of the Chinese "Anaconda"**

**Bibliographic Information
of the German National Library
(Deutsche Nationalbibliothek)**

The German National Library
lists this publication
in the German National Bibliography.
For detailed bibliographic data
please refer to: http://dnb.d-nb.de

IMPRESSUM

Copyright: **2011 Norbert Braun**
Printed and published by: **Books on Demand GmbH**
                                     Norderstedt
ISBN: **9 783842 357839**

CONTENTS

PREFACE

The Western industrial nations have fallen victims to the Asian "Anaconda" concept.

They are now in the position to develop their come-back out of a position of defeat and inferiority.

They have to re-develop a new basis of existence and living.

The Vietnamese concept is an impressive example how to build up a position of strength out of a position of total inferiority.

From a starting point of total inferiority they defeated two major military powers.

Could there be a better proof that creativity has no limitations ?

Success and victory can be developed from the most unlikely starting point.

We are all faced with superior forces in our daily life. An improved mastering and management of this situation can improve the quality of life considerably.

INTRODUCTION:

1 WAR ECONOMY -PEACE ECONOMY

China has turned her economical growth and the economy of the advanced regions into a war economy.

The labour intensity of a war economy provides China with an incredible advantage. They can achieve labour performances and efforts which are out of the reach of a peace economy.

It enables them to progress at a breathtaking speed to a rapid success. All obstacles which are in their way, are removed on the spot.

Germany had a labour force during the period of her economical miracle after the war that was used to repair the industry in bombarded regions overnight.

Her fighting force had to cope with enemies who were often twentyfold in armament and numbers.

Human efforts were tuned to a very high pitch. The achievement of economical results had total priority over leisure time and enjoyments of life.

Workers achieved performances which were impossible to achieve in peace economies. Germany's War Generals and Officers had turned into Managers of Industry. They often demanded a work intensity and efforts from their staff which no Manager would dare to ask for in a peace economy.

Above all, they had developed techniques and a state of mind to defeat opponents who were vastly superior in numbers and armament.

The battle of Kursk and other battles were always on their mind and drove them to outstanding achievements.

The next generation of managers had no background of war and making the impossible possible. So the war intensity disappeared. Working life became very normal again and returned to a peacetime performance.

The labour intensity of a wartime period was well observed and analysed by Chinese leaders. It fitted well into their very ambitious plans.

It became a key element of their success.

The German industrial achievements in peacetime were of very little interest to Chinese leaders. They had the ambition to become the research center and factory of the world.

The German wartime labour intensity was the missing link to their success which was going to turn a Western dominated world into an Asian dominated world.

The war intensity of an economy without firing a single shot is a unique revolutionary achievement.

It may change the world more than the two World Wars before. World Wars may be regarded as economical contests where only less intelligent participants spill blood to please an armament industry.

Chinese military history has had her own heroes in store who influenced Chinese thoughts and actions.

Sun Tsu was a key figure here.

The Chinese system has certainly 1.000 million discontented and neglected Chinese behind breezing down her neck.

These Chinese have been bypassed by the economical boom up to now. They represent a tremendous menace which forces them to an incredible speed.

They are running 2.000 m when the West manages modest 300 or 400 m.

The West is strong enough to survive under these conditions, but at a very reduced level. The shrinking process has already started.

It appears that the middle class is the first to be eliminated.

Is the Western population happy to live with a strongly reduced life quality which keeps on shrinking ?

I think the time has come to benefit from the strategies and the success story of the winners.

This creates the basis to make our own efforts towards recovering the lost life quality.

2 EVERY BONANZA HAS ITS PRICE

The ability to maintain a wartime labour intensity and speed of progress is an outstanding achievement. The ambition and desire of 1.000 million frustrated people is the fuel which drives them ahead. It requires miracles to avoid a very violent eruption or even a Ming dynasty-like change of power.

The economic victory against your opponent without any fight or bloodshed shows the true genius of the Chinese strategy.

We are obviously witnessing a masterpiece of economical warfare. In the end we are experiencing a new world with new rulers without having shed a single drop of blood.

Western industrialists know that their products are being copied. The copies stand next to the originals. They have to tolerate this development and have to concentrate on obtaining at least one slice of the total business.

There is no market which can take the place of the Chinese market. In the case of German car manufacturers, business even bypassed the turnover figures of their home market.

Honesty and decency die first in economial warfare. It is perfectly legitimate to build entire industries upon the developments of the opponent.

The exploitation of the weakness of the opponent is a very important element to final success.

A sense of human decency and compassion for the opponent is considered as a serious misconduct. The disgust against an armed contest is a very high principle.

SUCCESS

FROM THE POSITION OF INFERIORITY

ACCORDING TO SUN TSU

Generating success from the position of inferiority is, of course, the true challenge.

Anybody can produce success from a position of superiority. Winning from an inferiority base requires a far better planning, an extremely high degree of motivation, and an iron will to succeed over a long period.

This endless stream of creativity, human moral and motivation is likely to triumph over sheer strength. Clear objectives and the concept of final triumph and success must be in the mind of each challenger.

Temporary defeat must not break you, but immediately release an increased creativity.

Evolution has shown that the rich, scrupulous and mighty usually first win the upperhand.

Even the strongest appearance has its weak spots. These have to be recognized, analysed and exploited.

Exploitation of the weak points of today's champion is an important column in your final success.

Creative ways have to be concieved to sap strength from the strong opponent. A slight, but constant loss of strength can already change the tide.

It is very important that the opponent recognizes the discreet challenge only when it is too late.

1   SUCCESS NEEDS PRECISE PLANNING

Confidence tricks are the backbone of success in the exterior relationship - according to Sun Tsu.

Pretend to be inferior when you are in a position of strength.

Pretend to be without ambition when you are already absorbing the customer base of your opponent.

Success or defeat in an action can be recognized beforehand by the quality of precise planning. Every detail has to be considered.

You have to turn each useful development to your advantage.

Offer a bait to your opponent and pretend your own weakness and unpreparedness.

Always exert pressure on your opponent and do not allow him to recover.

Attack your opponent where he is unprepared. Defeat him where he does not expect it.

High speed action and progress is of great importance.

The opponent has to be totally unprepared for your final agression.

Ideally, he recognizes the menace only at the moment of the "coup de grace".

Make the opponent nervous and frustrate him.

Always consider the evolution and the present situation for your action.

Wisdom, honesty, tolerance, courage and discipline are the essential preconditions for success in the interior relationship and the customer relationship.

You have to subdue your doubts and have to realize your vision.

You have to understand markets and the fast changing technological and financial environment extremely well to initiate the correct actions.

For your direct and indirect plan of action you have to understand obstacles to foresee the likely development and changes.

2   PREVENTIVE ACTION

It is of importance to prevent that your opponent can realize his strategic plans.

To win against your opponent without fight or struggle is the work of a true genius.

A true genius can recognize and solve problems before they occur.

He can win against his opponent before a menace develops.

It should be your main objective to gain control over each item which is important to you.

With this strategy your success will be complete.

The opponent who knows when he has to make utmost efforts and when he should postpone his actions, is likely to win.

Know your opponent and know yourself, and you will win the contest.

If you do not know your opponent and yourself, you will experience great risks.

The cautious opponent who watches the development and waits for a favourable moment to uproot his overconfident opponent, will succeed.

Intelligence has never been mentioned in connection with long hesitation.

An action should take place at high speed.

Refinement is of secondary importance.

A professional opponent will protect himself against defeat. He cannot be certain of success. The vulnerability depends on the opponent.

Establish yourself in a position from which you cannot fail.

From this position, you can reach your objectives step by step.

You have to develop a long-term strategy and have to take the human factor into consideration.

3   SUCCESS BY SURPRISE AND PRECISION

When a falcon breaks the back of a pigeon with the energy of his flight, he uses the ideal timing.

To achieve a similar timing, is an important element of success.

From the position of considerable strength, you may pretend weakness and vulnerability, to lure your opponent to make mistakes which you can exploit.

Strength or weakness may be more or less the same.

The practical use is part of your overall strategy.

4   "POWER OF WATER"

Start the development of favourable opportunities when your opponent is totally unprepared. Attack your opponent where he does not expect a challenge. Avoid the strength of your opponent and defeat him at his weak spots.

Learn from the strength of water.

Water has a soft appearance, but succeeds in digging its way through mountains by forming canions and gorges.

Become flexible and irresistable like water.

You have to gather all available information on the strength and the weaknesses of your opponent and his friends and sympathizers.

You have to consider every item to ensure your success.

Your success is very much influenced by the careful use of your opportunities and meticulous planning.

Knowing the strength and the weaknesses of your opponent allows you to tune your actions as subtle as you hit an egg-shell with a hammer without damaging it.

The number of choices which you can use to uproot your opponent are as numerous as the five different tastes which allow millions of variations.

When a river moves big rocks, the changes are achieved by continuous pressure and motion.

5 UNDERSTANDING YOUR OPPONENT

A true master in advancing his personal success is always cunning and secretive. He does not leave traces.

With this art, you learn to be invisible and unperceived. That way you gain control over the fate of your opponent.

Always exploit a weak spot of your opponent. Hide any traces to prevent you from being discovered. Avoid any noise so that your activities remain totally unnoticed.

You will be irresistible when you exploit the weak spots of your opponent. You will always be safe if you move faster than your opponent.

Use the proverb: "Come like the wind, disappear at lightning speed".

A cunning opponent will force his will upon his adversary. He will not permit losing his advantage.

The opponent should never know where you shall start actions. This forces him to prepare a defence at many points. In each of these many points he will always have a weak presence only.

If the opponent expects a frontal confrontation, surprise him in the back.

If he protects his back, he will be vulnerable at the front.

Try to understand the intentions of your opponent. This will allow you to decide which strategy will succceed and which will fail.

Analyse where your opponent is vulnerable and where he is strong.

Always try to camouflage your actions. This will prevent your adversary from planning counteractions.

It is extremely important that nobody understands your strategy which will lead to your final success.

6   STARTING POSITION

In your contest with your opponent always make sure that you have the better starting position.

Keep away from uphill struggles. Arrange for the downhill advantage.

Do not let the decisive favourable moment pass by. If you do not act, it may take a long while to experience a similar opportunity again.

Do not act in periods which do not hold an advantage for you.

Always make sure that your back is well protected. Make all possible efforts to avoid attacks from behind.

Motivate your opponent to start activities which may risk his status and reputation.

Anything which weakens his position is to your advantage.

Avoid baits which are arranged by your opponent to destabilize your position.

It is very important to evaluate correctly the position and opportunities of your opponent.

Do not underestimate his chances. You may be the loser in the end.

You have to consider long-term strategies. This may cause a short-term disadvantage to win a long-term victory.

If your opponent is very honour- and reputation-oriented, you can harm him seriously by arranging for baits to shatter his reputation.

Morality is one of his weaknesses which you have to exploit.

If your opponent is easily excitable, he may not consider the risk and complications.

You have an ideal background to lure hime into a trap.

7 WEAKEN YOUR COMPETITOR

Always try to occupy a position in which you cannot be defeated.

Always be prepared for an action of your opposition and prepare yourself for a counteraction.

Even if your surroundings appear to be very peaceful, always expect negative activities behind the scenes.

Always use the opportunity to arrange for traitors to be employed by your opponents.

You will be well informed of all their actions and can arrange for skilful sabotage actions.

You have to undermine the position of your opponents from within.

If you want to strengthen your position, plan damage to your competitor.

You have to understand the action of your competitor in advance and consider the damage which may derive from these actions.

Do not endeavour for positions and advantages which you cannot defend in the long run.

Be very cautious when your opponent is already with his back against a wall. He may act unpredictably.

If your competitor or opponent is superior to you in position and strength, attacks in his back without his awareness are most reasonable.

Occupy something which is of key importance to your competitor or opponent.

This will irritate him and initiate that he makes mistakes which you can exploit.

8   THE DECISIVE BLOW

The most important success formula in a contest is the absolute superiority in speed.

Speed of progress is the decisive factor.

Exploit every advantage which derives from an unaware and unprepared competitor.

Develop potentials in totally unexpected areas and attack where the competitor is totally unprepared.

Prepare surprise attacks where he is unprepared and weak.

Use diversion and camouflage techniques to hide your intentions.

Make him feel nervous and insecure.

If your competitor has several unities, try to separate them.

Your opponents may be as tough as a snake.

If you beat their head, their tails will attack you. If you beat their tail, the head will attack you. If you hit their center, both head and tail will attack you.

Your actions and steps have to be unpredictable.

You have to leave your environment in the dark about your true intentions.

You cannot set up alliances before you know what your potential partners truly intend to do.

You must have precise information about the circumstances, background and condition of your competitors or opponents.

Develop the capacity to finish your opponent in one decisive blow.

Pretend the shyness of a virgin until you receive the chance to lance such a blow.

Act then with the speed of a running hare to ensure that your competitors and opponents have no opportunity to organize a defence.

USING SUN TSU WISDOM

FOR YOUR OWN SUCCESS

1 INFORMATION ABOUT COMPETITORS

Information is a key element of success. It is essential that you have precise information on the intention, plans and steps of your competitors or opponents. This enables you to counteract their actions before they endanger your existence.

To become a true master of victory, it is important to establish an information structure around your competitors. This keeps you informed on every move your opponent makes.

If possible, you have to defeat him before he can act.

This requires a thorough preparation to prevent damage. Pulling the strings in secrecy is considered as a way to success which is of religious importance.

You receive, of course, the information from people who work directly or indirectly for your competitors. Potential informants are those who have lost their jobs and those who have not been considered in promotion.

There is a sufficient number of persons who are doublefaced or change with the wind.

It is very important to recognize the persons who work for your competitors and who feed information to them.

Make them work for you. They know the secrets and weaknesses of your opponents.

To operate without agents and informants is like operating without eyes and ears.

Servants in the service of opponents have changed power and fortune in China many times.

It is often advantageous to change your tactics as often as a ghost may change his appearance.

2   TURNING MISFORTUNES INTO ADVANTAGES

A victory over a competitor has to be precisely planned. With detailed planning you can win. With careless planning you cannot win. An analysis of the planning can predict victory or defeat.

To win you have to know when to start your moves and when it is wise to postpone them.

Speed is the key element of success. Use the unawareness of your competition to your decisive advantage.

Chose selected areas of attack. Your competition will be in trouble because of being unprepared.

If the competitor is aware of your intentions, use preparing actions against him. He must not know where you will start moves. This forces him to prepare defence in many places. This will weaken his strength at any one point.

It is vital that you make efforts to disrupt your competitor's alliances to weaken his position.

One key reason of your actions is to turn misfortunes into advantageous situations.

Deception has to be an essential part of your strategy.

You should use the principles of water and its enormous concealed strength. Water is totally flexible and accepts the shape which the ground permits. You should act the same way and adopt this success formula of water.

Do not accept any rules and conditions. Follow your road to success.

It is important that your moves and actions cannot be predicted.

Never use the same tactics for a second time.

The most promising way of progress is to attack your competitors' strategies.

The next best solution is to absorb his alliances and to make them work for you.

3   MOMENTUM

You reach the highest perfection in eliminating your competitor or at least to subdue him without him realizing the contest.

You increase your own strength by absorbing your competitor's achievements intact.   You certainly do not benefit from destruction.

You have to time your decisive actions as precisely as a falcon who has to break the backbone of its prey.

Your Asian adversary will not act on the market principles we are used to.

You have to determine in which fields you want to compete. Do not allow your competitor to dictate terms of competiton.

You have to discover the agents who are paid by your competitor.

You need an excellent fore-knowledge of your competitors. This knowledge is required to produce a high quality plan to absorb your competitor or his sales network.

You have deserved high marks if you win victories because of your ability to adjust to the changing situation of your opponent.

To win you have to know and apply the direct and indirect strategies.

It is always beneficial to entice your competitor to underestimate you. You have to pretend to be weak if you want to benefit from your strength.

Beware of your opponent's baits. Do not succumb to them.

Deception is very vital in a contest with a competitor. If the competitor provides an opportunity, quickly capitalize on it.

Asian companies try first to gain a foothold in a new market. They try to maintain the momentum by pulling other manufacturers from the same national stable in.

This reminds you that the competitor is essentially the combined economy of a Nation rather than a single company.

The objective is to keep the momentum until the entire global market is under their control.

4   IMPOSE YOUR STRATEGY

Your road to success requires that you subdue personal emotions.

If you are sensitive to honour, you may over-react when being insulted.

If you are quick-tempered, you can easily be made furious.

Your compassion with people can easily be exploited.

If you act cowardly, you can easily be demoted or subdued.

If you act recklessly, you can easily be eliminated.

If you are already applying a useful strategy to subdue your opponent, you still have to adapt to the circumstances to make the best of your advantages.

It is wise to occupy a position of non-defeat and use every opportunity to defeat your competitor. To obtain a position of non-defeat, you have to create advantages for yourself all the time.

You will win if you are well prepared to seize every opportunity.

Evaluate your competitor's plans to determine which strategy will win and which strategy will lead to failure.

Assess the situation and then move.

You have to determine the fields in which you want to confront your competition.

You have to prevent that this key choice is made by your competition.

You have ensured your final success by the quality of your precise planning.

With your deep knowledge of your opponent and yourself, know the economic environment and the changes within your competitor, and your success will never be challenged.

A victory can be created. Even if your opponent is superior in number, you can prevent him from challenging you.

5   MAKE YOUR COMPETITOR A CERTAIN LOSER

To win a contest it is very important to anticipate correctly your opponent's plans and moves so as to defeat him right at the start of his new activities.

Your competitor must not be able to guess your next moves. He will expect your actions, but has no idea of what will happen. This will force him to defend himself everywhere and weaken his position. He will be weak at any one point.

You have to build up inner strength and fighting spirit to reach your objectives.

Move swiftly and try to uproot your competitor. Once you have gained the momentum make all efforts to maintain the momentum. It offers you the opportunity of decisive success.

Your competitor will not be able to touch ground for some time.

Build up solid ties to people who have similar interests and are likely to support you.

Pay attention to the points of strategic importance and make sure that developments are to your advantage.

To go for swift victory must be an essential part of your planning.

Avoid prolonged actions which may tie you down for a long time.

Win first against competitors who are easily to defeat and improve your strength.

Try to keep control over the development by planning the action and evolution first.

Avoid a head-to-head competition.

Try to become strong in areas which have been neglected by your competitors. That way you create a situation where your competitor is already defeated when a contest starts.

You win because you have created facts which make your competitor a certain loser.

THE INFLUENCE

OF SAMURAI TRADITION

ON ASIAN BUSINESS STRATEGIES

1   FOLLOW THE COURSE OF WATER

Asian nations can draw an amazing strength from their warrior and Samurai tradition.

They can produce an impressive intensity in the strategy of winning from their past wisdom. They prove that wisdom can still be very useful after many centuries.

One important proverb is:

"Follow the course of water and you are on the road to victory."

Not only do you have to consider your own individual position, but understand the larger context and draw benefits from the evolution.

You should not allow anyone to analyse your final intentions.

Maintain a relaxed inner attitude.

You have to recognize the menaces from your opponents in all their depth.

Do not become destracted by less important actions.

The intention of a Samurai-influenced competitor or opponent is always to eliminate you.

A destroyed competitor is a good opponent.

If you have experienced one success, you can challenge twenty similar competitors to claim world dominance in your industry.

You can involve other industries in the same field to benefit from the victory.

The key objective is to eliminate your competitors.

You have to concentrate on their very objective when you work out your detailed strategies.

2   DISTURBING STRATEGIES OF COMPETITORS

You have to anticipate that your competitor has done similar intensive planning work as you have done.

Your opportunity is to upset, disturb or even destroy his strategy.

Undermining his strategy systematically will make his plan collapse and create opportunities which you can exploit.

Create alliances who will provide you with significant leverage factors.

Forge alliances with trustworthy allies to tip the balance of strength in your favour.

Pay attention to the minutest details. They may open you the path to major opportunities.

It is very vital that you recognize and understand the facts and menaces which are hidden and concealed to you.

Develop the ability to understand a complex situation at first sight.

Learn to evaluate profit and loss with every project and development.

Train achievements and civilization of the Samurai, their deeply influenced Asian business strategies, progress and speed of action.

Famous Samurai like Musashi have deeply influenced the speed and intensity by which important objectives are pursued.

The top Samurai was proud that his body and his swords had become one tightly knit unit.

This created the decisive advantage essential for a long success story.

You have to use your ambition to survive and to head for success with the same intensity as a Samurai.

3   GET YOUR COMPETITOR OFF BALANCE

Many events can get people off balance. Sudden danger or unexpected difficulties can reduce the capacities of your opponent. In the off-balance awareness your opponent becomes very vulnerable. You can surprise him by attacking him at unexpected points. The advantage of the momentum glides into your hands.

You have the departing position to achieve final victory. You have to deny him the chance to breathe or to recover. You have to depart for victory in the most advantageous position for you.

You have to exercise this development frequently.

If you get involved in an extensive struggle with your opponent, try to apply the "melting-together"-strategy if you cannot achieve victory. If you cannot develop a success despite your intensive embracing strategy, intensify this condition even more. It gives you the opportunity to develop your final success strategy. That way you will win.

Train this and become very familiar with this strategy.

You cannot move heavy obstacles from the center. Try to develop your success from the corners. If these corners get lost for your competitor, he will lose strength considerably.

You must not abandon your momentum, but conquer one corner after the other. If you have conquered most corners, the opponent will get weaker and weaker and will finally give up.

You have to become expert and master of this strategy.

If you admire the strength and the well functioning organisation of your opponent, attack his unprotected sides and dig yourself in.

If you realize that he starts to collapse, withdraw and attack at another point.

Your activity resembles the zigzag-line of a mountain trail.

Recognize the fighting rhythm of your opponent. Then engage yourself with all your heart and maintain your position.

Keep this in mind and train the sequence as frequently as possible.

If you feel that your competitor has no fighting spirit, concentrate all your force in one decisive action and crash him. You have to prevent that your competitor recovers strength.

If you feel that you are stronger than your opponent, try to smash him with one decisive action.

Even if by applying these strategies, the competitor may give the impression of being defeated. Yet his fighting spirit may still be very active. The apparently defeated may be undefeated deep down in his awareness.

You have to change your strategy very fast and have to break the spiritual power of your opponent. You have to create the condition that he feels defeated even at the deepest levels of his awareness.

You have to activate all your strength to produce this decisive blow.

It is, however, not easy to verify the success of the action.

If your opponent loses his strategy and rhythm, he is ready to be defeated.

Your attitude should not be defence-oriented. There is a tremendous difference between attacking or being attacked.

You have to concentrate on the heart of your opponent. You have to find out his true inner strength.

Do not attack before you understand the true intentions of your opponent.

Do not act hastily, because you may create a situation where your success becomes very unlikely.

4   UPROOTING YOUR OPPONENT

You force your fighting techniques upon your adversary and force him to tune his ways to yours.

You have to train these strategies well and victory will always be yours.

Your objective is to lure your opponent through your actions into a difficult situation.

Your objective is to shatter his position. You have to force unexpected things upon him. This way he gets irritated and starts to break.

I have seen that Western Managers can be just as effective in applying Asian strategies.

Uprooting the opponent and absorbing his customer base is a very efficient road to lasting success.

There is no real difference in the strategies.

Some experts are of the opinion that the West will experience a period of decadence. They will lack the spiritual strength to defeat the Asian challengers.

A comeback is absolutely vital for long-term survival.

5 "THE FLOWING WATER-STROKE"

Decide to apply this stroke if you are at equal strength with your competitor.

If he decides to withdraw or step aride follow him with concentrated body and spirit and hit him first like letting the water of a barrage of water escape, slowly at first, but then with ever increasing speed.

You have to develop a way which enables you to eliminate your opponent with great skill.

Do not underestimate skill and strength of your competitor.

6   "THE ROTATING STROKE"

This stroke allows you to injure all sections of your opponent's body with one single stroke.

This stroke you should train very intensively, because it is frequently applied.

You will understand this stroke in an intensive contest.

Your opponent will be out of action if you have hit his head, arms and legs.

7   "THE STONE AND SPARKES-STROKE"

This stroke requires that you are equally strong with body, arms and legs.

After your blade has hit the sword of your opponent, keep on striking with all your strength without lifting your sword.

You have to train this well - several actions in one fast sequence.

8   "THE DOUBLE HIP-STRATEGY"

The subtle use of Japanese and Chinese fighting techniques and strategies makes the Asian industrial development more dynamic and more successful than the Western approach.

Body and sword have to melt together to one acting unit.

In modern times, your business has to become a part of yourself.

With the relentless improvement and further development of your success strategies, you become a true master of your skill and profession.

The inner attitude to improve your skill and professionalism day by day will make your superiority so overwhelming that your competitor loses a bit of a chance on a daily basis.

Ceaseless training provides you with the unbeatable craftsmanship.

Defeat your competitor in one decisive stroke. Apply the action with utmost speed.

You apply this strategy, if you recognize that your opponent is still undecided and needs to make up his mind.

If your competitor withdraws after your attack, strike back immediately in a mock attack.

This "double hip-strategy" is not easy to apply and needs thorough practice beforehand.

If your competitor prepares a stroke, you may perform a stroke without imagination or thought.

This is an important strategy which requires intensive training.

9 "THE COLOUR AND GLUE-STRATEGY"

This is the winning strategy by which you stick to your opponent.

You never separate from him.

Head, body and limbs remain as close as possible to your opponent.

Prepare yourself carefully for this strategy.

10   "THE   POSITION   OF   CHINESE   MONKEY-STRATEGY"

The position of Chinese monkey is a strategy by which you leave your arms close to your body.

You approach your competitor. Before he can strike, you are in close touch with him.

Rush with closed body towards your opponent. This way you get close to him.

You have to practice this strategy as often as possible.

Your body turns into a long sword, or the long sword becomes a body.

Usually you move body and sword to eliminate your opponent.

You can start by fighting your challenger with your body first, before you start sword action.

You should always start with the sword first and let the body follow.

Train this strategy carefully.

HOW TO APPLY THESE STRATEGIES

FOR YOUR OBJECTIVES

Your personality and your business objectives have to melt together to one well functioning unit.

The intensity of your action must exceed any Western-style effort by far.

The Samurai tradition obliges you to eliminate your competitor. Co-existence is not part of tradition and system.

This makes the situation very straightforward.

Your survival is at stake, no more, no less.

If you have analysed that your opponent is inferior, you should use the opportunity to reach a decision with one decisive action. Deny him the chance to recover.

Avoid to repeat strategies which have not been successful. Change your strategy as often as it is required to achieve success.

If the opponent thinks of a mountain, attack him like the sea. If he thinks of the sea, chose the mountain approach.

Always advance in an unpredictable way.

Your opponent may have an enormous fighting spirit and may be difficult to defeat.

You have to become one spiritual unit with your body and weapon. Penetrate your obstacle with one spiritual stab to achieve your spiritual target.

If you get entangled with your opponent, forget your plans and intentions and start afresh.

That way you discover the path to victory.

You should have sufficient fighting spirit to dominate and subdue your opponent.

Understand the position and standpoint of your opponent and imagine to be in his place. You start to understand his problems and shortcomings and realize step by step that his chances are considerably smaller than yours.

You start to understand that he is the pheasant, and you are the powerful falcon.

Analyse your true overall position, analyse the background of your competitor, analyse his qualities, his strength and weaknesses.

Your strength has to overcome the apparent advantages.

Every competitor has his rhythm, his speed, his strategy of defence.

Impose your strategy upon his, and you gradually win the required superiority.

You have many ways to defeat him. Plan this very carefully.

It is essential for your success that you recognize each of your opponent's actions and that you prevent him from executing you.

You have to be as close as possible to your competitor so that none of his actions escapes your attention and your preventive measures.

Analyse well if your opponent gets out of rhythm. This may announce his coming breakdown.

You have to corner your competitor so that he cannot escape.

If you miss the loss of rhythm, you allow your opponent to recover which makes your life unnecessarily difficult.

Try to prepare one decisive action to settle the contest once and for all.

LESSONS FROM GREAT MASTERS

TO TURN TIDE AND FATE

1   FREDERICK THE GREAT
(FRIEDRICH DER GROSSE)

Frederick the Great was ruler of a rather small German state. He was constantly faced with giant states like Russia, and Austria / Hungary who were after his skin.

Each of his opponents was vastly superior to him. With his superior strategies and tactics he managed to defeat them again and again.

His opponents were 30, 40 or 50 times superior in number and arms, but never managed to achieve final defeat.

Frederick proved to be an indestructable motor who managed to recover after every defeat.

He proved that with a small, but extremely well trained, motivated army one can achieve miracles. Frederick achieved an endless chain in military achievements and motivation which was near to miracles.

You can learn from him even today that victory can be achieved in the end if you never give up. With constant creativity you prevent your defeat. The table will gradually turn in your favour. Nothing is final. The influential factors are changing all the time.

You have to try to shape the events in your favour. Deception and bluff of your opponents may give you temporary advantages which may ease your situation.

Frederick may give you inspiration in this vast field. If victory cannot be achieved in moments which are unfavourable, get out of the way. Tomorrow the sun may be shining again in your favour.

2   FIELD MARSHAL GUDERIAN - YOUR MUSASHI OR SUN TSU

Germany's fate was that she was mostly confronted with a great number of opponents. This was due to the political constallations. Being confronted with opponents most of the time who were superior in numbers and equipment, German leaders had a tremendous challenge to think of strategies to defeat opponents who were often 10 or 15 times superior in numbers.

Field Marshal Guderian proved to have an outstanding talent to defeat superior armies and to uproot them. Once they were destabilized, he seized the momentum and kept it in hand until the final success was ensured.

Guderian was once faced with the combined French and British armies in the North of France.

Guderian had the habit of driving in the front line to discover opportunities which could be exploited.

He succeeded in destabilizing the two confronting armies with his fast tank troops. He made extreme efforts that the two armies remained destablilized and that they did not succeed in getting their feet on the ground again.

He would have succeeded to eliminate the two armies if less capable Generals from the Head Quarter. would not have been carried away by their ambition. They took the action out of Guderian's very capable hands and introduced stupid strategies instead.

Guderian proves that with the right strategies you can win against superior opponents.

Guderian had the outstanding capacity to make the impossible possible.

This capacity is important when developing the customer base of stronger competitors.

Guderian had the gift to identify the weak spots of the opponents and to use these opportunities immediately.

He combined creative imagination with dynamic energy. These talents created astonishing opportunities and surprising results.

Each employee who develops his virtues and applies them, will achieve amazing results.

Guderian has uprooted an opponent and driven him for hundreds of miles. The opponent was vastly superior in number and equipment.

Better concepts, better strategies, audacity, the extreme high degree of motivation of all people involved turned the disavantages into advantages.

Guderian is a shining example of how the underdog can defeat superior forces.

Guderian and Musashi had similar human qualities. Both were true Masters in their fighting and war discipline. By the true mastership in using all available means, a superior opponent had no real chance.

Guderian was a true Master in the recognition of the weak points of the opponent. All efforts and strength were concentrated on these weak spots.

The weak spots turned into a disaster, and the opponent could not prevent a negative development. He did not get the time or opportunity to recover.

The momentum of the collapse in the weak spot area was maintained and cleverly exploited. The temporary turmoil of the opponent was used immediately, and his rangs were destroyed and disorganized. The opponent was not allowed the opportunity to recover.

The configuration of destabilization was of key importance. The momentum had to be maintained to create the utmost damage and feeling of defeat with the opponent.

Guderian has the potential to serve as your Musashi or Sun Tsu.

Contrary to the Chinese and Japanese, the Germans did not wish to benefit from their military traditions. They decided not to set up an effective defence and counter-attack strategy.

Guderian was a shining example in the exploitation of the momentum.

E.g. there were no tarmac roads in the operation area of tank groups. Guderian enforced to make full use of the limited sunshine period to reach the good roads to the sea. This had to take place before the start of the mud period.

For your economic life, you can learn that you have to make full use of all economic changes. The time window for each success has to be fully used. It will often be decisive for you and your progress, and competitors have to be observed full time. Career opportunities will develop which have to be exploited immediately. Make full use of the momentum. Never allow it to pass by. Use it to its full extent.

Guderian used the momentum of his "Blitz"-attacks in masterly fashion.

Whenever he had a momentum under his control, he did not allow his opponent any chance to get his feet on the ground again.

His objective was to achieve a domino effect.

He achieved the "Blitz"-conquest of large regions. "Blitz"-attacks allowed him to gain control over opposition fortresses.

Guderian used the surprise momentum. These successes broke the backbone of his opponents.

For your personal use, you have to find weak spots in the defence of your opponent which allow the creation of a domino effect sequence. This has to be very carefully planed and executed.

As soon as weaknesses of your opponent become apparent, the momentum has to be implemented.

The domino effect has to be passed on to other parties of the same group. The competitor has to be destabilized so that he loses control.

You have to plan these successes and implement them with great care. You have to take every point into consideration to ensure a successful outcome.

3   HANNIBAL BARKA - AN OUSTANDING EXAMPLE

The West is rich in examples where underprivileged and inferior people have trimphed over superior opponents.

Hannibal Barka was such an outstanding example.

He proved that Rome could be defeated over and over again.

His father had already developed "Blitzkrieg"-strategies. That way they adopted the family name BARKA (lightning)

Hannibal's troops were always vastly inferior in number. His strategies to overcome this inferiority were often brillant and always highly intelligent.

He succeeded in wiping out entire Roman armies.

Unfortunately, rivalling families hated each other deeper than the enemy. Short-sightedness caused their downfall. They destroyed the only man who could save their skin.

So the final outcome was the trimph of treason over human decency.

Political rivals turned shining success into disaster. They lacked the vision that their sabotage would end in their own calamity.

Yet Hannibal shows that the creativity of the human mind can work miracles.

4   MOSHE DAYAN - ANOTHER SHINING EXAMPLE

Moshe Dayan is another shining example of how to win victories out of a position of obvious inferiority.

Strategy and creativity made the difference.

His strategy was to uproot his opponent and to cause him to flee. Once he was on the run, Moshe maintained the momentum. The opponent never received a chance to get his feet on the ground again and to organize a defence.

Speed was the key element of his successes.

At the start of the Yom Kipper War, the united Arab forces started action with one million troops, 5.000 tanks and 1.000 war planes.

Moshe Dayan had the better quality of people. They had a superior fighting spirit. Despite of heavy losses in the beginning, they persevered and defeated their opponents.

Moshe Dayan's strategies played a decisive role. He had a deep understanding of the opponents' mentality and their most likely steps.

The quality of his understanding the opponent and his ability to maintain the defeat momentum, made the difference between victory and defeat.

For your strategy, it will be vital to understand your opponent, his mentality, his connections and his intentions very well.

Once you have uprooted his position, maintain the momentum until your final success has been achieved.

5   KEMAL ATATÜRK -
THE FATHER OF MODERN TURKEY

Kemal Atatürk is another shining example of how to win from inferior positions.

He was often faced with fighting the British, French, Italian, Greek, Armenian, Australian and New Zealand armies at the same time.

His opponents were vastly superior in number and equipment. He divided them and defeated them one after another. He performed one military miracle after another.

His soldiers were even better trained than the best armies of the British Empire.

Atatürk always came up with some bright ideas to turn certain defeat into shining victory.

His opponents were dedicated to finish him off. They started immediately to kill all Turks and Jews if Atatürk's troops were not around to defend their lives.

Even by using very superior arms like battle ships, Atatürk always managed to turn the situation in his favour. He was the only Turk who could defeat that many armies.

You can learn from him that with creativity you can turn the most desperate situations into your favour. You will never be defeated. There is always a way out.

Kemal Atatürk was a champion in splitting an overpowering problem into many much smaller problems. These could be solved much more easily one by one.

This may be a very useful strategy for you.

Due to Atatürk's incredible achievements fame and power came automatically his way.

He always had a wider environment in mind, far beyond his immediate objectives.

His outstanding achievements made people green with envy. They already held the dagger in their hands ready to stab it in his back. Thirteen of them were caught in such an attempt and made close contact with the hangman.

From this you can learn that you better do not expect gratefulness, but have to find your personal way to success.

6   GENERAL VO NGUYEN GIAP -
   A LEGENDARY FIGURE

General Giap became a legendary figure. He proved that not all is lost when being challenged by superior forces.

Creativity is the opportunity to master much stronger challengers.

The unusual confrontation between the most modern and best equipped army in the world and troops of barefooted soldiers made the victory totally certain. The Vietnamese could not be a match for the US supremacy. General Giap arranged for transport on jungle trails. His troops disappeared underground. They dug even 25 km long tunnels which led directly under the US Headquarter. They could blow up the US Head Quarter whenever it appeared advantageous.

With these moves, he neutralized the vast superiority of his opponent and started to turn the tide in his favour.

He booked one battle after the other in his favour. He was certainly motivated by revenge since both his wife and child perished in a Hanoi prison. General Giap had no military training. He was a teacher and farmer by profession.

His moves and strategies could not be predicted by the cream of the US military academics. He remained an enigma which gradually led the US military cream to the guillotine.

This was the absolute trimph of the underdog.

You can achieve astonishing results if you apply his strategies and techniques on your scale for yourself.

7   GENGHIS KHAN - CHINA'S NATIONAL HERO

Genghis Khan is a national hero in China. From the Mongols, he receives a god-like devotion.

The great Khan is a fine example of succeeding from the position of inferiority.

He started as a slave and gradually became the Master of half the world.

His conquests have never been savage actions of wild horsemen.

Genghis Khan was always faced with opponents superior in number. With ingenious creative concepts he turned his disadvantage into an advantage.

His campaigns were masterpieces of precise planning and preparation. He took great interest in the strength of his opponent and the thickness and quality of the city walls. He arranged for the right artillery to gradually turn the city walls into rubble.

He was one of the Fathers of Chinese intelligence. With the quality of the work of 100 to 200 intelligence agents he became Master of half the world.

Today we are confronted with 800.000 Chinese intelligence agents. They are on the way to control the entire world. They are a tremendous challenge in the art of preparing success.

You have to reach and endeavour for a level of intelligence and preparation which was never required in the past. If you examine this challenge in detail, you will discover opportunities which you can develop and exploit.

DAWNING OF A NEW ERA

1   CHINA'S LONG HISTORY
   OF TECHNOLOGICAL SUPERIORITY

By exploiting the raw materials of the former colonies in exchange for new industries and infrastructure, China becomes as strong as the entire West.

By learning their culture, civilization and languages, China acquires a strength which the West never had. The West will soon become dependent on them for the supply of many raw materials.

China has been the leading technological nation for centuries. The expression **"Empire of the Center"** was justified. Now they are on the way to reclaim this position.

This time they will be stronger than any nation in history. Their strength in technology, cash and raw materials will force the West to become satellites step by step.

The Chinese are aware of the superiority of their civilization and believe that superior civilization as well as technological and industrial leadership represent an irresistable mix.

US-born Chinese claim cultural leadership and refuse to use any English word.

Their endless chain of industrial victories will sooner or later make them succeed in replacing our Western mind.

The Chinese strategy to concentrate all companies of a new industry in one area accelerates progress and competitiveness. A lot of time gets wasted if an industry is distributed over an entire country. The exchange of information is much faster in a restricted area which is specialized in one field.

2   THE RAW MATERIAL CHAMPION

Our world is changing at a fast pace. Change is particularly strong in Asia, Latin America and Africa.

Here the Chinese make good use of the enormous funds which they have earned from the West by securing the land and sea mining rights from the many nations which are mostly in need for cash.

The raw materials from land and sea are used to build new Chinese-controlled industries. They provide many industrial jobs for the local population and increase life quality. That way they become potential customers for Chinese electronic goods.

Politicians and Entrepreneurs have a high regard for European quality and professonalism. They insist in getting them at Chinese prices.

Chinese wage levels gradually become world standard.

This will turn our lives upside down.

To speed up progress and to achieve astonishing growth rates, the Chinese use the intensity and energy of a war economy in peace times.

This strategy makes the Western approach of Hot War obsolete. The Chinese win economic wars without spilling a drop of blood.

Their strategies are very efficient, but they are not strategies of co-existence or of a peaceful world. The Asian approach is totally different.

We have to understand these strategies and develop new strategies which ensure economic survival.

3   USE OF WARTIME ECONOMIC SPEED

The wartime intensity and speed of China's industrial progress changes their world at an enormous pace.

We have only seen the beginning of the emerging industrial giant.

At this pace of progress mistakes like the Yangtse dam are inevitable.

Of course, it is an impressive ambition to construct the largest City of the world in the middle of China.

It makes sense to extend the construction of new industrial cities from the coastal areas into the central regions of the country.

The industrial mega cities of Chungking, Shanghai and Wuhan require a fast growing supply of energy.

China is, perhaps, working at twenty mega projects at any one time. We have to accept that not all of them are successful.

The Chinese take our future industries away from us and leave it to us to make a decent living without our bread and butter-industries.

We have to learn to take industries away from the Chinese.

Until then the West will be an eternal loser.

4   TSUNAMI OF INDUSTRIAL EXPANSION

German industry has considered the solar industry as a worthwhile industry to gain world dominance.

Germany had received an order from China to build the largest solar cell factory in the world. The fulfilment of this order proved to be suicidal. The Chinese realized the potential of the solar industry. The Chinese Government decided for the construction of 6.000 solar factories.

This tsunami of industrial expansion proved to be lethal for the German industry.

The Chinese industry realized the German dream. They will do it again and again. With their war-like industrial intensity they will always be the winner.

Other proud industrial nations can only hope to get some crumbles which fall off their table.

They refuse to reserve industries to the West. The industrial survival of the West will not be guaranteed by the Chinese. The West will have to make considerable efforts for every piece of existence.

Chinese industry and Government have already changed the life of every industrial employee in the West enormously. In the future, their decisions will dominate our lives.

It is becoming very important to understand their very different way of thinking and actions.

Their strategies have reduced Western industries to the role of the eternal loser.

5   FACTORY OF THE WORLD

China has achieved her objective to become the factory of the world. Her industrial work force is so vast that factory production could entirely become a Chinese responsibility.

The rest of the world has to find new ways to earn a living.

The next evolutionary step of the Chinese will be to become the R&D Department of the world.

They know that the present world contest is decided by industrial strategies and the creativity of an army of engineers. They have built up this army. They can concentrate entire aereas on industries with great future potential. These will become the world centers of their industries. The concentration on restricted areas accelerates progress and evolution.

Every Western worker and employee has to find his or her place in this emering new world.

He or she has to understand the success strategies of his or her Asian counterparts and absorb those which will be useful to him or her.

Many of the industrialists he or she has worked for before, have become opponents.

This increases the need for independent acting and thinking.

Small, independent, creative solutions will be in great demand.

Working in factories will be an Asian privilege.

6   THE SHORT-CUT OF GLOBAL LEADERSHIP

China's Authorities have implemented an economy with a warlike performance. This enables them to set up a solar industry with 6.900 manufacturers from nowhere and claim global leadership.

The real investors lose confidence confronted with such a tsunami.

Anyone who criticizes this selfish conquest of new business potentials is punished under military law and is declared a traitor. Punishment can be at leat three years of severe imprisonment. His chances to spend his whole life in prison and labour camps are excellent. The most trivial reason can extend his prison sentence for several years.

I once witnessed the impressive results of these war-style business performances.

A smaller roller bearer manufacturer in Southern China explained to me that his objective was the conquest of the customer base of the almighty German roller bearer industry. It sounded to me as if a mouse planed to swallow a tiger, and I could not hide a smile.

A decade later he was on the way to achieve his objective.

The German industry was badly shaken.

A Sales Director of the German roller bearer industry explained to me: "They work relentlessly on our customer base. They have our client list and do not leave anyone out. They attack our customer base in good times or in difficult times with changing concepts."

This relentless intensity was irresistible in the end.

7   COMPETITORS' CUSTOMER BASE AS A PRIME TARGET

Today we experience the speed which Asian national organisations apply to absorb the customer base of a Western competitor. These successes are the result of long-term objectives and a very detailed plan to achieve these objectives. When they start, they have the manpower ready to start developing business in 30 to 40 countries simultaneously.

Western companies are not used to this excellent planning and preparation work.

German industry operated in a similar way in the decades after World War II. They were managed by Officers from World War II. The use of "Blitzkrieg"-strategies was very natural to them.

I have experienced that competitors asked for mercy. The new sales strategy had uprooted them, and they realized that they were losing their customer base at an astonishing speed.

The economic miracle had these strategies as its basis. Audacity, courage and high speed were the secrets of the German economic miracle.

China and Japan still draw on the virtues and discipline of their military tradition. Germany decided not to use hers. Military virtues were totally out of fashion.

Japanese Managers were astonished and even disappointed that Germany left entire attractive industries to the Japanese rather than to benefit from similar military traditions.

If the Germans would have built up Guderian as a Musashi-like figure, many industries could have been defended and millions of jobs saved.

As one Chinese General explained 2.000 years ago:

"The best battles are won without spilling a drop of blood. This is the most effective way of military and political sucess."

The Chinese Authorities have implemented a very clever and intelligent way to be the eternal winner with the philosophy of Sun Tsu.

They can move and advance at breath-taking speed.

With these strategies to pinch all new industries with great production and employment potential from the West, the West will collapse in the end.

Guderian had developed the military conquest to an art and used his passion as a driving force.

With the same passion, today's Managers have to advance the conquest of competitors' customer base.

8   NATIONAL MARKETING STRUCTURES

The German industry did not follow the shining Japanese example.

Many sales and marketing training and service companies of many nations took advantage of the booming German market.

They implemented their companies' policies.

There was no institution to form and implement a national success structure and formula.

9   INDUSTRIAL INTELLIGENCE SERVICE

Today the Chinese Institutions employ 800.000 industrial spys. They have the task to make all industrial secrets available to China.

Such a tremendous army of industrial spys are like a cloud of grasshoppers which only leave an industrial desert behind them wherever they have been active.

To this number you have to add a similar number of Managers who work for the Chinese for hard cash and thus become traitors to their employees.

When a company gets infiltrated by corrupt Managers, the Chinese undermine everything which is directed against them. At this stage, a defence becomes always impossible.

Changing the Chinese partner is no protection against espionage.

Organisations like the China Development Corporation and others will make the search available to all industrial parties in China. You are not faced with private Western-style countries, but with a gigantic industrial conglomerate which has an impressive distribution system of industrial secrets.

The industrial secrets of the German solar industry have been made available to 6.000 potential competitors.

A German success story with many new jobs was turned into a Chinese success story.

10   PROMOTING BROTHERHOOD
IN INTERNATIONAL INDUSTRIALISATION

The Chinese have the sales and marketing structure to develop business with global players in more than fifty countries simultaneously. This creates mega business. A Western company may need decades to build up similar structures. This creates an enormous growth potential.

China has paid great attention to secure the supply of oil and raw materials. They took advantage of the arrogance of the former colonial powers. They made good use of the tremendous financial strength which they had accumulated.

Most Governments preferred to discuss business with the Chinese rather than with their traditional colonial powers.

The Chinese took the exploitation of raw materials at sea and land in their hands and delivered entire industries and a modern infrastructure. They often turned up with a workforce of 100.000 engineers and specialists.

The Chinese Government was interested that this workforce lived together with the natives. They learned their language, culture and mentality. China did not waste any money on international hotels.

They preferred to promote brotherhood with many countries.

The strategy to supply entire industries in exchange for the exploitation rights of oil and other raw materials proved to be extremely popular. It opened the industrial world up for many emerging nations. Step by step the Chinese acquired the exploitation rights for entire continents. This will provide them with a tremendous advantage in a world with dwindling oil resources.

The availability of oil will force many countries to enter in alliance with China in the interest of their own survival.

11   THE CHINESE WAY TO PROSPERITY

China is developing the new industries of Asia, Latin America and Africa in all discretion. They create tremendous business potential.

These continents are still receptive for Western products and technologies. They want them at Chinese prices. This is a decisive condition.

This development will turn our lives upside down. The good old Western way is obsolete and has its place in our impressive industrial museum.

We have to absorb success strategies of the Chinese and the way of thinking of their conquering classes.

These have to be used so we can find our place in a new world.

The Chinese use their rich military tradition to gain important competitive advantages.

They bring business competition to a new level. They are effective enough to bring Western competitors into a losing position right from the start.

In the contest between Kain and Abel, Abel was full of virtue, but he was doomed right from the beginning.

Kain shaped our world. We have to absorb this wisdom.

12   IS THE WEST TURNING INTO AN OPEN-AIR MUSEUM ?

Chinese tourists love to visit Western countries. Nothing much happens there. There they realize the charm of giant open-air museums. They find societies that approach economic standstill. It is easy to become disheartened if the Chinese copy any new industry which you develop and sell at prices which you can never reach.

No matter how difficult the challenge is, the West has to survive and to learn to compete with superior opponents.

When comparing Western Officials with Chinese Officials, the Western decadence becomes apparent. The Chinese are far more result- and performance-oriented.

The decline of the British Empire was mainly caused by the decadence of her population. The British had the courage and honesty to talk quite openly about it.

The West must show the same virtues. We have to analyse the situation honestly before we can introduce steps to overcome the problem.

The disastrous air and water pollution which makes the common population of China suffer, will most likely be solved faster than the West has overcome its pollution problem of the war time industry.

The first significant steps to turn this into a giant business opportunity can already be recognized. China needs all globally available resources to produce and buy enough food for her 1.4 million people. To achieve this objective, a new world will be created in which we have to find our place.

SURVIVAL IN A NEW WORLD

1 THE GLOBALISATION OF THE CHINESE WAGE LEVEL

For many families, it becomes more and more complex to earn a living. The value of labour is falling down to Chinese level.

China is even further reducing her wage level by transferring her production to Egypt or Indonesia. This reduces the wage level to 25% of the previous level.

You have to consider that you cannot feed a family with an industrial wage anymore. You have to add a business income to your wage to offer your family a decent living.

The Internet allows you to look for business in the global village. This requires, of course, a very professional operation in this vast community.

The newly prosperous countries will not welcome you as a job applicant. They have to give priority to their own mass employment.

The modern wage level will make it extremely difficult to offer a decent living to a family.

You have to be as creative as our ancestors to organize a good life quality from a number of income sources.

In the time of our ancestors, a painter was expected to design and build a beautiful castle. Many of these outstanding achievements were created on the basis of **"learning by doing"**.

The construction of gothic cathedrals with their ability to survive earthquakes and bombings are a shining example.

2   THE WAR-LIKE LABOUR EFFORT

Today, it is almost impossible to build success on comfort and the sweetness of life.

I was surprised to realize that the public institutions in China were open at 2.00 c'clock in the morning.   In Hong Kong, you were offered business opportunities at 2.00 or 3.00 o'clock in the morning.

The abundance of fine food was the paradise on earth for Chinese people.   They were rewarded for their midnight visit in a fine restaurant.

Millions of their countrymen who starved under Mao Tse Tung's political moves, made them aware how important fine food was for their survival.   They were always prepared to make hard work sacrifices for a piece of paradise.

Germans were prepared for sacrifices in a similar way.

I remember the words of Guderian to his troops after an outstanding achievment:

"I have asked you to go without sleep for 48 hours. You have marched forward with very little sleep for 17 days.   Your opponents attacked you from behind and from the sides relentlessly. You have never been disheartened or shaken.

With masterly self-confidence and the deep conviction in the successful completion of our mission you have mastered all tasks with deep dedication."

3   THE MIRACLES OF ECONOMIC WARFARE

Today you depend on the emphasis the national marketing institutions are placing on your industry and its growth potential. They may leave it to one or two companies to compete with you. They can just as well decide that a province of 80 million citizens has to live by the potential of your industry.

You could be faced with an industrial avalanche of an industrial superpower. In this case you will have a real challenge for your creativity.

The Western-oriented world was relatively comfortable. It was easy to find your place. The age of industry is continuing in China. In our world it will be fading away. Our industries are celebrating their successes in the booming countries.

It is very vital to always be in the winning camp.

It is certainly essential to collect all available information on all Chinese activities in all parts of the world. This involves:

1   **New industries**
2   **New oil exploitations off-shore and on land**
3   **New mining activities**
4   **All infrastructure activities (roads, motorways, railways, water supply, energy projects, etc.)**
5   **Investments in existing companies to gain control step by step, e.g. Greek port installations.**
6   **Investments in financial institutions**
7   **Strategic investments in industries to acquire know-how and customer basis**
8   **Localizing the clandestine efforts to transfer further industries to China.**

It is certainly a worthwhile effort to collect all available information on the present projects of the Chinese global activities in Europe, the former European colonies, the two Americas, Asia and Australia.

You will end up with a few hundred projects.

The Chinese activities, particularly in the West, are often very secretive.

According to the Chinese military philosophers, the prey should not realize the threat before the "Coup de grace".

4   THE CHINESE MARKET

Chinese industry competes with Western business in every interesting industry. No volume activity is left out.

The half-price Chinese strategy is very popular with the dwindling purchasing power of Western work-forces. They have to purchase Chinese products since their purchasing power does not give them any alternative. This accelerates the decline of companies which cannot operate globally due to limited resources.

I do not think that the Chinese market is more difficult to develop than the US market.

Chinese make the starting period often rather easy and comfortable if you have something interesting to offer. You have to be useful to their strategy and their long-term plans.

You have to remember that they are hungry for jobs. 1.000 million Chinese demand the same progress and improvement of life quality that 400 million Chinese already enjoy They put pressure on their Government.

Western industries expected a gigantic solar boom in China. This was a realistic assessment. The boom is already developing at full speed. They launched, however, 7.000 Chinese companies and ensured that this new financial current was to the benefit of China.

The original inventors experienced frustration and deception. They have to look for business elsewhere.

Above all, the Chinese have created and initiated a tsunami of competitors.

5   YOUR CHANCES IN AN ASIAN AGE

Step by step the Asian age replaces the European age. It happens at a much greater speed than most people anticipated. Our precious Western-style life will gradually fade away.

The time has come that we have to tune ourselves to the new age and start to develop opportunities for ourselves.

You must not postpone it for too long. Your best chances may be taken by others, because you did not compete.

Every industry and occupation will be subjected to enormous changes. In many fields, the situation will be turned upside down.

Some industries will be totally transferred to Asia. In these cases, nothing may be left in your home country. You have to develop a new way of life.

You have to analyse the evolution and development in your occupation and industry. It pays to make the first steps to build a new future at an early stage.

The traditional emigration countries have lost entire industries themselves. You may change one challenge against another without adequate social protection.

When extreme mega cities of the size of New York emerge, the tax and income situation may change to a very difficult evolution.

You may have to finance major medial operations or treatments entirely yourself.

A sufficient income will be an absolute essential requirement.

6   TURN THE ASIAN AGE TO YOUR ADVANTAGE !

You have a moral obligation towards your family and yourself to turn a difficult development into your advantage and into a positive evolution for you.

You have to understand the Asian objectives and plans and try to occupy positions which fit in with your aspirations and intentions.

China had the ambition to become the factory and the R&D Division of the world. Today they have almost realized their dreams.

This evolution has changed the financial currents enormously. They are the financial basis of the enormous economical progress of China. They have enabled China to secure the oil and raw material sources of many countries and oceans. They are replacing the influence and the economical basis of the West.

A Chinese world is gradually emerging.

With the changed financial currents they have acquired enormous funds. They can build entire industries in developing countries payable with oil and raw materials off-shore or on land. They do not need to insist on cash for payment as the Western countries do.

They create many industrial jobs in countries with considerable financial difficulties. They create a strong economical basis for decades or even centuries.

All this is financed by the new Chinese industrial conquests. The punishment for losing will really hurt at a later stage.

7   ADAPTATION TO A NEW WAY OF LIFE

Most of the great fortunes have been made in economically difficult times.

You have to implement unusual concepts which reflect your creativity.

Asian countries grow richer at the expense of Western economies. It is a slow, but steady decline. There may be periods of financial improvement.

China is always quicker to exploit the potential of new industries. There is a great potential in exploiting the decline of family fortunes and companies. Hundreds of thousands of small companies and members of professions will disappear. They leave a wealth of equipment and furniture behind them.

You may find customers for the second-hand equipment in the developing countries.

People may cling to their homes and departments as long as possible. They dream of living in their home at the age of retirement.

Particularly at retirement age you will need sources of income which you will find in areas of intensive commercial activity.

People have to be highly mobile. Immobility becomes a dream of another age.

You may find a steady income in finding and developing these homes and offices which have been built at the wrong place. Offices can be used by companies which depend on communication with the outside world rather than on site.

8 WITH GREATER EFFORTS AND WORK INTENSITY YOU WILL REACH YOUR OBJECTIVES

The new directions of financial currents have changed the world. Today the richest nations of the world like California pay with "I owe you's" and the hope that one day you will receive payment.

China and Japan control a money tower. The business people of world dream of participating in these money towers.

The newly rich like the Chinese have started to buy desirable Western products like German cars, French wine and brandy, French and Italian fashion, etc.

There is a great opportunity to develop a market in Asia for the products of your own or your employer. You have to apply the same creativity which Asians had to develop to succeed in our markets.

They were often totally exotic to them and required an enormous degree of adaptation.

Creating bestsellers is anything but easy. I have seen product developers cry because their products were rejected again and again.

There was, however, the iron will to create bestsellers and to be extemely successful. After many efforts they arrived at bestsellers. Once they had achieved these victories, their success stories never ended.

It is, of course, not easy since the riches of this world have moved to the other part of the world. They will probably never return.

You have to accept that much greater efforts of complexity and work intensity are required to reach your objectives.

Today's technological level allows you to earn your income globally.

This is not money which comes easy your way.

You have to labour your field with great intensity and dedication before you can enjoy an abundant harvest.

EPILOGUE

Today we are at the beginning of great economical revolutions which will change our way of life in the years to come.

The Chinese have secured the raw material resources of entire continents like Latin America or Africa. Great emphasis is placed on off-shore exploitation. They have paid great attention to the world's off-shore resources and built up the necessary know-how.

The Chinese have secured 120.000 tons of the 124.000 tons of rare metals which have been produced this year.

Many advanced technologies are already at the Chinese mercy. The Chinese can already eliminate their competitors at their discretion.

More and more industries will depend on Chinese raw material supplies for their survival. This will promote the immense financial resources of China even further.

Today the Chinese dispose of 2.9 billion US-$ of foreign currency resources. The fortunes which the US and other European countries had accumulated after World War II, have found their way to China and today are almost entirely in Chinese hands. The Western industrial countries control only 10 % of the Chinese wealth.

This is only the beginning of a long-term development. It is overdue today that China co-operates with the US in the financial and economical management of this world.

Step by step China will claim her future role as industrial and financial leader of the world.

This will be a different world as the Western countries used to know.

Everybody is well advised to develop his or her role and extra income in this new world.

The potential of the Western economy may dwindle and is certainly not sufficient to maintain the accustomed quality of life.

BIBLIOGRAPHY

1	Sun Tsu Die Kunst des Krieges	WBG Darmstadt 2008
2	M. Musashi Das Buch der fünf Ringe	Econ Verlag GmbH Düsseldorf und Wien 1983
3	Hannibal	Heyne Biographien München 1980
4	Moshe Dayan Story of my Life	Sphere Books Ltd. London GB 1978
5	Peter Brent The Mongol Empire	Weidenfield and Nicolson Ltd. London GB 1976
6	General Vo Nguyen Giap	Biography Free Military History Newsletter

ABOUT THE AUTHOR ...

Norbert Braun - Certified Industrial Interpreter for English and French, Certified Accountant for Industrial Production, Sales Trainer and Sales Promoter - has been entrusted with very difficult sales missions in many countries around the globe. His outstanding achievements made him "Mr. Mission Impossible" on the sales sector.

In his first book **Die Kompostierung der "Grufties" und "Scheintoten" (Composting the "Buried" and "Nearly Dead")** he describes a Japanese working initiative in which he participated and whose objective it was to create working places for senior people.

Furthermore, he was entrusted with the task of selling Computer-based Learning Software (CBL-SW) to the HQs of Labour Exchanges, Ministries of Labour, Ministries of Science, Regional Administrations and Educational Institutions. This happened at the time of the re-union of the two Germanies, when many people had to be re-trained to the working methods of the West. After that a follow-up business was arranged, preferably in countries with great employment problems, such as China, Russia, Australia, Canada, Northern Spain, France, Great Britain and Ireland.

In his first book, the Author places his know-how and rich experience at the disposal of the inhabitants of dying economic regions as well as employees and workers of migrating industries in order to enable them to re-conquer a part of their lost standard of living.

In his book **"Bruttosozialglück statt Raubtierkapitalismus" (English version: "Gross National Happiness versus Predatory Capitalism"),** the Authors offers a way how to achieve a higher quality of life by changing established values.

In his present work, the Author explains how to develop success and victory out of a position of total inferiority.

FURTHER WORKS OF THE AUTHOR

1
Die Kompostierung der "Grufties" und "Scheintoten"

**Ein visionärer Versuch,
wertvolles Humankapital
zum Leben zu erwecken**

**(A visionary attempt
to restore precious human capital)**

2
Bruttosozialglück statt Raubtierkapitalismus

**Ein Versuch,
der wirtschaftlichen Götterdämmerung
des Westens entgegenzuwirken**

3
Gross National Happiness
versus
Predatory Capitalism
(English Version of 2)

**An Attempt to Counteract
The Western Economic
"Twilight of the Gods"**